Is that a ...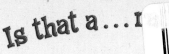

From where Benjamin was standing, he could see the brown-and-black diamond pattern on the snake's skin. When he pulled out his binoculars and focused in, he noticed that the snake was coiled in such a way that he could just see the rattle at the end of its tail, looking like a line of plastic beads. He could also see its hooded black eyes— looking right at him!

"Is it, uh, poisonous?" Gabe asked, concerned.

Benjamin looked at Gabe and said, "We need to ask my mom."

Gabe was frozen to the spot. "Mom," Benjamin said as calmly as he could manage. "I think I see a rattlesnake."

JEFF CORWIN

JUNIOR EXPLORER SERIES: BOOK 3

THE WILD, WILD SOUTHWEST!

Illustrations by Guy Francis

PUFFIN BOOKS
An Imprint of Penguin Group (USA) Inc.

To Maya, Marina, and Natasha

PUFFIN BOOKS
Published by the Penguin Group
Penguin Young Readers Group,
345 Hudson Street, New York, New York 10014, U.S.A.
Penguin Group (Canada), 90 Eglinton Avenue East, Suite 700, Toronto, Ontario,
Canada M4P 2Y3 (a division of Pearson Penguin Canada Inc.)
Penguin Books Ltd, 80 Strand, London WC2R 0RL, England
Penguin Ireland, 25 St Stephen's Green, Dublin 2, Ireland
(a division of Penguin Books Ltd)
Penguin Group (Australia), 250 Camberwell Road, Camberwell, Victoria 3124, Australia
(a division of Pearson Australia Group Pty Ltd)
Penguin Books India Pvt Ltd, 11 Community Centre,
Panchsheel Park, New Delhi - 110 017, India
Penguin Group (NZ), 67 Apollo Drive, Rosedale, North Shore 0632, New Zealand
(a division of Pearson New Zealand Ltd.)
Penguin Books (South Africa) (Pty) Ltd, 24 Sturdee Avenue,
Rosebank, Johannesburg 2196, South Africa

Registered Offices: Penguin Books Ltd, 80 Strand, London WC2R 0RL, England

Published by Puffin Books, a division of Penguin Young Readers Group, 2009

1 3 5 7 9 10 8 6 4 2
Copyright © Jeff Corwin, 2010
Illustrations copyright © Guy Francis, 2010
All rights reserved
Printed in the USA

LIBRARY OF CONGRESS CATALOGING-IN-PUBLICATION DATA IS AVAILABLE.

Puffin Books 978-0-14-241440-8

Printed in the United States of America

Dear Reader,

Before my family moved to a rural part of Massachusetts, I grew up outside of Boston, where I wasn't always able to explore the natural world. So I had to find unique ways to discover the animals and plants around me—which led me right into my backyard! Even though I was living in a city, I found lots of amazing wildlife right outside my door. I just had to take a closer look!

And that's what the Baxter kids like to do in my Junior Explorer series—explore their immediate surroundings. Whether in a desert or in their hometown near the Florida Everglades, Lucy and Benjamin Baxter always find ways to discover fascinating animals and plants. And so can you! It doesn't matter where you live—all you have to do is look outside, engage your curiosity about the natural world, and have fun discovering the plants, animals, and natural life around you.

Happy exploring!

Jeff Corwin

JEFF CORWIN
THE WILD, WILD
SOUTHWEST!

Chapter One

Benjamin Baxter unzipped his backpack and took out a carefully folded map. He spread it out across the ground in his family's campsite in New Mexico, anchoring each corner with a big rock so it wouldn't blow away. "Lucy! Gabe! Come here!" he shouted, calling his sister and his cousin over to take a look. "The Gila National Forest," he said as they approached.

He swept his hand over the map dramatically. "Our home away from home!"

Lucy studied it until she found the place where they were standing, a small campground near the middle of the park, nestled beside the West Fork of the Gila River. She pointed to the spot, showing her cousin. "Okay,

Gabe, imagine a red arrow in this area. It would say, 'You are here.'"

"That's what it says on subway maps," Gabe said cheerfully. He'd lived all of his nine years in Brooklyn, New York.

"Not on a map of a national forest, though," said Benjamin. "Here they make you figure it out yourself. Luckily, I had plenty of time to study it on the plane."

"And while we waited to rent a car. And while we drove here from the Albuquerque airport," Lucy added. It had been a long trip, but they were finally here, with still a few hours before it got dark.

Gabe nodded. "It's good that you're an expert because, you know, I'm not." He had never been camping before, but this summer the Baxters had talked his family, the Sullivans, into joining them for a trip. Ever since they'd been to visit Gabe in New York, the kids had been dying to see him again. And after their trip to the city, their parents had been eager to show Aunt Lily and Uncle Peter the wonders of living in the great outdoors. Right now, the grown-ups were hard at work setting up the tents a few feet away.

Benjamin squatted next to the map, a stick in his hand. "So the park is in the southwest corner of the state," he said, pointing. "Not far from the Mexican border."

Lucy glanced over at her brother, rolling her eyes. "Don't mind him while he recites the guidebook from memory," she told Gabe. "The rest of the trip will be a lot more fun."

Benjamin smiled, but he didn't stop. "Hey, this is important stuff! The Gila covers more than three million acres of land, and includes two wilderness areas where there aren't even any roads. People think of New Mexico as a desert—and a lot of it is—but most of this park is mountains and forest. It's home to a variety of species. Which means . . ."

"Lots of different animals?" Gabe broke in, proudly. When the Baxters were in New York, they spent a lot of time looking at local wildlife. Gabe had learned a lot.

"Yes!" cried Lucy. "The forest is full of all kinds of creatures we've never seen in person."

"Like what?" Gabe asked, a mix of excitement and concern in his voice.

Benjamin didn't even know where to start. "Well, definitely lizards and snakes. Maybe even mountain lions..."

"Mountain lions!" Gabe said with alarm. "And there's just going to be a tent between us and their teeth?" He was so loud that the grown-ups could hear him, and his mom and dad looked up with concern.

Beth Baxter, Benjamin's mom, stepped away from the tents for a moment and took a long drink out of her water bottle as she walked over to the kids. "Don't worry, Gabe," she said when she reached them. "I doubt there are any mountain lions in the immediate area." Mrs. Baxter was a scientist who studied animals. "They're reclusive creatures, anyway—they tend to steer clear of people. Nothing to be concerned about." She smiled Benjamin still hoped to catch a glimpse of a mountain lion, but the Sullivans looked relieved. Maybe Gabe and his parents were more nervous than he'd realized.

"We're almost done here," said his dad, Sam Baxter, hoisting a tent to an upright position. "The tent poles are in—all we need to do is stake them into the ground and then we can start moving in!"

Benjamin folded up his map, and they all moved over to their tents. He couldn't wait to set up his stuff. The grown-ups would have one tent, while the kids would have another one beside it, all to themselves! It would be like a big slumber party!

"Could you kids get some water? The bathrooms are down that path," Mr. Baxter said, pointing, "and I think there's a water pump down there, too."

Hoisting three large water jugs, the kids set off together. Gabe and Lucy ran ahead, but Benjamin lagged behind for a few minutes, looking around the campground and taking it all in. The area was in a sort of valley, with mountains stretching up all around. He could hear the soft rumbling sound of the Gila River, too, coming from behind a row of trees at the edge of the campground.

"Hurry up," Lucy called. As much

as Benjamin wanted to explore, they had to finish setting up camp before it got too late.

Up ahead, Gabe and Lucy found the water pump. Lucy pumped the handle, and water dribbled out of a spout. "Your dad must be really thirsty," Gabe commented as they filled the second gallon jug. The Baxters looked at each other for a minute, baffled, until Lucy started to giggle. "This isn't just for him to drink," she said. "It's for all of us! We'll use some of it for drinking, and some will be for cooking and cleaning."

"And for my nice hot shower?" Gabe asked dryly.

Benjamin wasn't sure if he was joking. "Some campgrounds do have showers," he said. "But this one is pretty basic. It just has some outhouses and water pumps, plus a couple of picnic tables. If you leave the water out in the sun, it gets warm, though. We could try to rig up a shower . . . ," he said, trailing off.

"I was kidding!" Gabe said. "I don't know a lot about camping, but I know

I'm going to like the getting-dirty part of it. Who wants to waste our visit taking showers? We can do that when we get back home."

Benjamin gave his cousin a high five, while Lucy grimaced.

"So what do you guys do on camping trips?" Gabe asked as they finished filling the jugs and headed back to their site with the water.

"Go hiking, mostly," said Benjamin. "That's what our parents call it, anyway. I like to think of it as exploring. There are tons of trails, and if we get tired of that, there's swimming in the river and just hanging out in our tent."

"The best part is at night," Lucy said. "It's when you feel most connected to nature. In a place like this, the only light will be from the stars and from our fire, and the only sound will be from animals, wind, and water. Trust me—it's amazing!"

It was starting to get dark, and they heard a bird calling as they walked back toward their tents. Benjamin wondered if it might be a hawk.

"Animals? Do they come out to hunt at night?" Gabe asked, sounding worried.

"Well, nocturnal animals come out at night," Benjamin said. "But other animals hunt all day long." He saw Gabe's concerned face. "But the thing is, none of them are hunting us. They may want our food, but our parents will put it where they can't get it. Like my mom said, there's nothing to worry about. Really!"

Before Gabe could reply, they were back at the campsite. "We're moving in!" said Aunt Lily, poking her head out of the grown-ups' tent. There was a pile of gear on the ground, and Benjamin's mom was coming up the path with another armful of bags.

Benjamin turned to his cousin. "You've never slept in a tent before, right?" he asked.

"Never even been inside one," Gabe confirmed.

"You're the first one in then," Benjamin said, looking over at Lucy, who nodded in agreement. That meant that Gabe would get to pick the least lumpy spot on the ground for his sleeping bag, but the Baxters were willing to give that up. If their cousin had any worries about sleeping outside, it would definitely help him to have a comfortable place.

Feeling generous, Benjamin watched his cousin open the tent flap and crouch to get inside. Then, with surprise, Benjamin watched him pop back out and run to the other side of the site, as far from the tent as he could get. "Seriously, I think I'd rather stay in a hotel," he said, his voice shaking. "There's a lobster in there!"

Chapter Two

"What? No way!" yelled Benjamin. When he looked into the tent, he saw why Gabe was a little freaked out. It wasn't a lobster—it was a scorpion! The creature was small and brown, about as long as a pencil, with crab-like claws and a long, segmented tail curving upward over its body. Benjamin wanted to get a closer look, but he knew that scorpions could sting. He was pretty sure a grown-up would have to help.

"Mom," he said when she arrived with the last of the stuff from the car. "There's something you need to see in here."

Beth Baxter dropped a backpack in the dirt, opened the tent flap, and peered in. Then she pulled her head back out and started rummaging through a nearby bag. "I don't want to take any chances," she said, holding up a paper cup. She headed back into the tent.

"It's definitely a scorpion," Benjamin's mom stated as she walked out of the tent with the creature in the cup. "And some of them are extremely dangerous."

Gabe took a quick look at it, then took several steps backward.

"Should you even be this close to it?" Uncle Peter asked, joining the group.

"It's okay," said Mrs. Baxter. "Scorpions are from the same group as spiders. They use these claws to catch insects or small rodents," she said, pointing to them. "And then they sting the prey with their tails. The tails contain a poisonous venom that will paralyze or kill the prey, depending on the kind of scorpion. In very rare cases, a scorpion's venom can be fatal to a human. If I was stung by this one, though, the effect would be basically like a beesting."

Gabe shuddered. "It's . . . creepy," he said.

"I'm sorry you think it's creepy, because they like the dry climate of New Mexico. Chances are, we won't see another one. Still, it's a good idea to shake out your shoes before you put them on. Scorpions sometimes hide in them for shelter!"

Gabe grimaced. "I think I'll be

keeping my sneakers on every night," he said. "Just in case!"

After the kids searched the area around their tent for more scorpions —and found none—they started to settle in. They unrolled their sleeping bags side by side and tucked important belongings, like flashlights and guidebooks, in the tent pockets. Then the families built a campfire, roasted hot dogs, and made gooey s'mores— melted chocolate and marshmallow oozing over graham crackers. "Can I have s'more?" Lucy joked as she finished her third.

As the fire crackled, the parents explained the plan for the trip. They would spend two nights in the Gila National Forest, then drive across

the state to the White Sands National Monument and Carlsbad Caverns. "New Mexico has mountains and forests, deserts and vast caves," Mr. Baxter said. "While we're here, we'll try to see as many of these different wildlife habitats as we can!"

Lucy, Benjamin, and Gabe smiled with excitement as they headed into the tent and settled down in their sleeping bags. It was getting late, and the three cousins fell asleep as soon as their tent flap closed, lulled by the sound of the river moving by and dreaming of the adventures that lay in store for them.

Benjamin woke the next morning to the sound of scuffling outside his tent. He thought it was an animal at first, but when he peeked through the tent's window, he could see that it was Aunt Lily, trying to get the fire started again. He climbed over his cousin and his sister, crept out of the tent, and whispered, "Can I help?"

"Sure," Aunt Lily said, smiling.

Benjamin showed her how to stack the wood so it would catch fire, and then he stepped back and let Aunt Lily light the match.

A few minutes later, Gabe and Lucy came out of the tent together, rubbing their eyes. Gabe looked up in wonder. "I can't believe we're outside!" he said. Benjamin knew just what he meant. He loved waking up in the outdoors, feeling the early-morning cool and quiet of the woods.

After a quick breakfast of instant oatmeal, the kids got dressed. Benjamin couldn't wait to venture deeper into the forest, but the grown-ups seemed to linger forever over their coffee. Instead of waiting, Lucy asked permission for them to explore down by the river while the parents got ready for a hike. "Just as long as you are careful and don't go in the water," Mr. Baxter said. "And you should take these," he said, handing her a walkie-talkie that they used for camping trips. "If you need anything, just radio back here for help."

"Okay," Benjamin said, leading the way toward the riverbank at the edge of the campground. From here, he had a sweeping view of the forest. There were tons of trees, of course, but it was unlike anything he'd seen back home. Everything was green and lush in Florida, but here the trees, mostly pine, were surrounded by scrubby undergrowth and dry ground. Only the riverbank seemed moist and muddy.

And then, as far as he could see, there were warm red outcroppings of rock jutting into the air. Some of them were as tall as small buildings! The landscape reminded Benjamin of something he might see in an old Western movie, rough and unsettled.

He could hear Gabe's footsteps squelching behind him. "Do you guys always get to do this?" he asked. "Just wander around? This is the best! My parents are too nervous to let me wander around by myself at home."

Lucy said, "Our parents get nervous, too. But the walkie-talkies make them feel better, and they want us to get out and see things on our own."

Gabe nodded and smiled as they approached the river. Then he pointed suddenly. "Look! I see fish in the water!" He wasn't afraid this time—just amazed.

The river was as clear as a swimming pool and, now that Gabe had pointed it out, Benjamin could see that it was thick with fish. "Wow!" he breathed. He didn't know what kind they were, but he'd never seen so many fish together in one place, even when his family was watching salmon spawning in Alaska.

He flipped through his guidebook until he got to the section about the Gila River. "I think they're trout!" he called to Lucy and Gabe. The trout looked coppery, with irregular black spots on their sides—they might even be the famous Gila trout! These trout were being crowded out of the river by other, nonnative trout, Benjamin read, but scientists were trying to make sure the population of Gila trout could continue to grow.

"Benjamin, come on," Lucy prodded, walking ahead with Gabe.

"But there could be more animals around here." He continued to skim through the guidebook. "Did you know that some frogs live close to the desert?"

He glanced up and could hardly believe his eyes.

"Hey, look!" Benjamin pointed. A frog was right there, watching him!

"Is that a frog?" Gabe asked, turning around and looking where Benjamin was pointing.

Benjamin scanned the book to see if he could identify it. "Actually . . . no. It's not a frog at all! It's a red-spotted toad!"

Lucy and Gabe hurried over to him. "How do you know?" Gabe asked.

"They're about two inches long, and olive green in color, like this one," Benjamin said. "But the giveaway is the red warts all over its skin! See them? They're small and bright, and almost the same color as the rocks!"

Before they could take a closer look, the toad hopped away in several giant leaps.

The kids scrambled a little closer to see where it'd gone, but it was too fast for them. And just then they heard their parents' voices filtering through the walkie-talkie, calling them back. It was time to begin their first hike of the trip.

Mr. Baxter led the way down a path to the Gila Visitor Center. "It's the only one in the whole park, and our campsite happens to be near it," he said. "It will be a good place to get our bearings and find out more about the park."

As soon as the two families entered the center, a man in a brown uniform approached them. "Can I help you?" he asked. "I'm a ranger at this station."

Mrs. Baxter said, "We're looking for some trail maps, if you have them."

"No problem," said the ranger. He showed the grown-ups a rack with dozens of maps. Then he turned to the kids. "So, are any of you interested in signing up for our Junior Ranger Program?"

He happened to be looking right at Gabe, who didn't know what to say. "M-maybe," Gabe stammered. "But what does a ranger do?"

The forest ranger smiled. "Well, we do two important things. We help visitors while they're here, giving them directions and safety tips and other important information to make sure everyone enjoys the park. And, at the same time, we protect the forest *from* the visitors! Rangers teach people how they can visit without harming the environment around them and how they can help preserve it for visitors in the future."

"So they're the experts," Lucy clarified. "They're scientists, tour guides, guards, and teachers all at the same time."

"And we can become rangers, too?" Gabe asked, sounding confused. "Scientists, tour guides, and all that? I'm not sure I really know enough—"

"Well, you'd be *junior* rangers," said the ranger, chuckling. "And you don't need to know anything to start! The point of the program is that you learn while you are here." He took out a booklet and explained, "In this guide booklet, there are activities and games to do as you explore the park. They'll help you learn about what you're seeing here—the wildlife, the plants, the rock formations, and more. When you've worked your way through them, you bring the booklet back here and have it checked. If you've done a good job, you'll be sworn in as a junior ranger. You'll get a certificate and even a badge!"

"Well," said Gabe. "I've learned a lot already . . . I'd like to make it official!" Benjamin and Lucy nodded in agreement.

"Here you go," the ranger said, handing each of the kids a booklet. "Hope to see you back here soon—ready to join the ranger team!"

The kids tucked their booklets into their backpacks as the families prepared for their hike.

"Are you ready to see some caves?" Mrs. Baxter asked excitedly. They'd be heading along a winding trail, taking the long way to the Gila Cliff Dwellings, some spectacular caves at the bottom of a cliff where the Mogollon people had made their home about seven hundred years ago. "I know you kids are interested in seeing animals," said their mom, "but trust me—you will be amazed by these caves."

Benjamin's parents led the rest of the family down a path so narrow they could only go single file. He knew to stay close to the group, but Benjamin hung back at the end of the line on purpose.

He fished his junior ranger booklet out of his bag and opened it. One of the first activities was to draw a "sound map," or a picture of one place based only on the sounds you could hear instead of the things you could see.

Benjamin waited for somebody to stop ahead of him, and when he saw Uncle Peter rummaging through his bag, he took advantage of the moment. While everybody else was waiting, Benjamin closed his eyes and began to listen.

Of course he could picture what was around him—he'd been taking it all in as they walked. A twisting river, a steep canyon carved into red stone, some kind of pine trees dotting the hills. He knew the area around him was teeming with life, too, but he couldn't hear very much. The stillness around him was almost startling. It was hard to imagine how he'd draw anything with only sound to guide him.

Just as he was about to close his booklet, he heard what sounded like a chirp, or like fingernails against a blackboard. He opened his eyes, looked only at his booklet, and drew a small bird in a pine tree. When he finally looked up, he was shocked to discover that he'd been listening to a magnificent golden eagle, perched on a red cliff above him!

Benjamin stared at its sleek dark body, noticing the shiny golden feathers near its head. It was one of North America's biggest birds of prey, watching and waiting for its next meal, looking every bit as intimidating as the bald eagles he'd seen in Alaska. Benjamin would have said the sound came from an ordinary sparrow, yet it came from a bird almost as big as a condor! It was like his dad was always saying: Nature is full of surprises.

"C'mon, Benjamin. Stop holding up the hike," Lucy shouted.

Benjamin quickly closed his booklet and ran to catch up with everyone. Nature may be full of surprises, he thought, and so was their trip to the Gila National Forest.

Chapter Three

The temperature had risen steadily in the hour since they'd left the visitor center, and the sun blazed down as everyone made their way over a rickety wooden bridge. "Hang on," said Uncle Peter, pausing when they reached the other side. "I need some more water."

Benjamin was happy to have a break. He was getting hot, too. But he was pretty sure the cliff dwellings were coming up, so he reached for the map in his back pocket to make sure. That was when Lucy clutched his arm and pointed to a shady spot under a nearby pile of rocks. "What's that?" she asked. Benjamin looked and saw something smooth and shiny lying there, all coiled up.

"A snake!" Benjamin replied. He'd wanted to see one on this trip, but he hadn't expected to find one so soon!

From where Benjamin was standing, he could see the brown-and-black diamond pattern on the snake's skin. When he pulled out his binoculars and focused in, he noticed that the snake was coiled in such a way that he could just see the rattle at the end of its tail, looking like a line of plastic beads. He could also see its hooded black eyes— looking right at him!

"Is it, uh, poisonous?" Gabe asked, concerned.

Benjamin looked at Gabe and said, "We need to ask my mom."

Gabe was frozen to the spot. "Mom," Benjamin said as calmly as he could manage. "I think I see a rattlesnake." He pointed out its hiding place to her.

Uncle Peter dropped his water bottle.

"What?" he said, looking around. "Right here?"

"It's a good twenty feet away," Mrs. Baxter assured him, never taking her eyes off it.

"I read in my guidebook that most rattlers are about four feet long," Benjamin chimed in. "And they can strike only at a distance about half the length of their bodies, so we're not in the danger zone."

"But if there's one, there could be another one nearby," Gabe pointed out.

"True," said Mrs. Baxter. "But rattlesnakes won't attack unless they are provoked. Like all snakes, they detect predators by sensing vibrations in the ground, and their first instinct is always to hide."

"What about when they are hunting? They don't hide then, do they?" Gabe asked.

"They don't hunt people!" said Benjamin. He knew this from his reading, too. "They hunt mostly rodents, and they have an awesome built-in detection system. They locate prey by flicking their tongues in and out, sort of tasting the air. They can also detect heat from warm-blooded animals, which allows them to hunt in the dark. They're not going to mistake us for mice, I promise!" He smiled.

He hoped he was reassuring his cousin. He didn't want the Sullivans' first camping trip to be their last!

"If you respect them, they will respect you," Benjamin's mom said. "But we don't want them to mistake us for predators, either. There could be more snakes in the brush as we approach the caves, so let's all be careful where we step."

They continued walking, and in just a couple more minutes the group turned a corner and spotted the first of the caves they'd come to see. As the families climbed higher, they could see a string of them, hollowed out in the base of a gray-white cliff. "These are amazing," Lucy said.

"Aren't they?" a female voice replied.

Lucy turned around to see a ranger smiling at them. "Hundreds of years ago—before Europeans came to North America—these caves were home to the Mogollon people, a group of Native Americans."

The ranger led the Baxters and the

Sullivans through the caves and along the narrow catwalks that connected them. "We believe that these caves were homes to forty to sixty people," she said, "sometime in the 1200s. Around the year 1290, though, we think a drought forced the Mogollons to abandon them and look for new homes north and east of here. Experts aren't certain, though, since the Mogollons left no written records."

The largest cave was divided into several "rooms" by stone walls, and there was even an upstairs!

"Look!" Gabe said to Benjamin. "Here's where they made their fires for cooking." He was looking at a pit in the cave's rock floor.

Benjamin's eyes traveled upward, to the blackened ceiling above it. "And look! There's where the soot gathered," he said, pointing.

The ranger showed them where the Mogollons had conducted their traditional ceremonies. Then they climbed a rickety ladder to the upper level of the cave, where the Mogollons slept and stored things. Benjamin wondered what it must have felt like to live here. He loved camping out, but he wasn't sure this was quite the same. What would it be like on a cold night? he wondered. Or in a thunderstorm?

The ranger reminded the group that the Mogollons didn't have much in the way of conveniences. "Where would you get things if you had no stores?" the ranger asked. "You'd have to make everything by hand. And you would need to use the materials around you:

the plants, rocks, and animals right outside your door."

Gabe looked around. "But what could you use a bunch of rocks and leaves for?"

"Well, the yucca plant, for instance, was used in many different ways. The roots were baked and eaten, and the fibers in the leaves were woven into baskets and mats."

Benjamin liked the sound of that, the way the people relied on nature to meet their needs. Whatever they made was organic, recyclable, and sustainable, long before anyone even used those words!

Before their tour was over, Lucy poked him in the ribs. "Look!" she said, pointing to the side of the cave. Benjamin and Gabe walked up to the wall to get a closer look. Somebody long ago had carved a picture into the wall: a snake!

"That is called a petroglyph," the ranger told them. "We don't know exactly how it was made, or when, or by who. But rock art like that can show us what daily life was like for the people who lived in these caves."

"So snakes were a part of their daily life?" Gabe asked. "Maybe something they were worried about?"

"Possibly," the ranger said, smiling.

"I know exactly how they felt," Gabe said wryly. "Some things never change!"

In the afternoon, the families decided to break for lunch, and the kids pulled out their junior ranger booklets. "What do we need to do next?" Lucy asked.

"The next activity is to find some yucca plants," Gabe said. Benjamin looked around and right away spotted the long, spiky leaves with short stems that the booklet described growing close to the ground. Benjamin did a quick sketch of one in his booklet—

they reminded him of the palm leaves he'd seen around his home back in Florida. "In the springtime, they grow purple blossoms, then bear fruit," his dad said.

Benjamin was putting the finishing touches on his drawing when he heard Lucy suddenly gasp. He turned his head and saw exactly what had surprised her. "Hey, Dad, look at this," he said in a loud whisper. Basking on a rock, in the bright sun, was a Gila monster! It wasn't moving, but its bright colors made it hard to miss.

It wasn't really a monster, but a large, scaly lizard that Benjamin had never seen anywhere but in a book. He moved a little closer—but not too close. The creature was big—longer than a phone book and almost as fat as a can of soda. It had a black body and beaded scales in a colorful pink-and-orange pattern. It was definitely not trying to camouflage itself!

Mr. Baxter quickly looked away from his map and in the direction that Lucy and Benjamin were pointing. "Wow!" he said. Benjamin knew his father was as excited as he was. They all put their fingers to their lips at the same time, as if it were a secret for just the three of them to share.

"They usually live underground," said Mr. Baxter softly. "They come out only to eat—which they do about six times a year—and to take in the sun, which is what this one is doing. This allows them to store up heat."

This is amazing," Lucy said, as she

pulled out her camera and started taking pictures. Benjamin could hardly wait to show the creature to his cousin. But first he had to know one thing. "Aren't they dangerous?" he asked his dad.

"Yes and no," his dad replied. "Their bites are poisonous and painful—unlike snakes, they latch onto their victims, and it can be difficult to release their grip. But they bite only when provoked or when killing prey. And they move very slowly, so anybody who saw one coming would have plenty of time to get out of the way."

Benjamin looked over at Gabe and wondered what to do. His cousin seemed to like exploring, but he had been a little freaked out by the scorpion and the rattlesnake, and this would be the third venomous animal they'd seen in two days.

But how could he keep a Gila monster to himself?

Chapter Four

Making up his mind, Benjamin called, "Gabe!" and his cousin's head snapped up from his junior ranger packet.

"What is that?" Gabe asked as he eyes focused in on the lizard.

"I never thought I'd see one of these face-to-face," Lucy said excitedly as she put down her camera.

"It's a Gila monster," Benjamin told

his cousin, showing him. He left out the part about the poison venom—Gabe didn't really need to know that.

Gabe looked at him for a minute. "Wait a minute. Aren't those the ones that hiss?"

Benjamin had left out that part, too. Gabe knew more than Benjamin had expected! He had to admit it was true, though. The Gila was famous for opening its mouth as wide as it could and hissing at creatures that tried to corner it.

Gabe watched the Gila monster for a moment, as if he was trying to make up his mind about it. "Wow," he said eventually, shaking his head. "That is totally awesome!"

* * *

They spent the rest of the afternoon hiking and, after they stopped for a snack, finally made their way back to the campsite. Benjamin noticed that Gabe was looking around at the plants, insects, and animals on their walk back. Benjamin felt pretty sure his cousin was impressed by their first full day of exploring the Gila National Forest. He couldn't wait to branch out into other parts of the park!

That night, though, a heavy rain soaked their campsite. "Just our luck to get trapped here during a storm," Lucy grumbled inside the tent. They moved their sleeping bags to the center of the tent to avoid the rain that was dripping in from the sides. "It hardly ever rains here."

The kids played card games by flashlight until bedtime. "What if it's raining tomorrow?" Gabe whispered after lights-out.

"We put on our rain gear and carry on," Benjamin whispered back. "My parents always say we can't let a little bad weather ruin a trip." But just then, thunder started rumbling. Benjamin knew that while rain didn't bother his parents, lightning did. They always said that there was no safe place to be outdoors during a thunderstorm. Sure enough, a few moments after lights-out, all four grown-ups were at the tent opening just as a jagged bolt flashed across the sky. "Come on, kids," said Aunt Lily. "Everyone into the van."

When both families were crammed inside, his dad made an announcement.

"I really hate to do this," he said. "But I think we're going to need to cut our trip to the Gila a little short. There are thunderstorms in the forecast for tonight and all day tomorrow. So . . . I propose we move to Plan B."

"Plan B?" asked Benjamin. "But we haven't become junior rangers yet." His mom gave him a look, but he didn't care. He didn't want to leave!

"Instead of camping here tonight, we'll drive across the state to the White Sands National Monument," his mom said. "We'll spend the night in a motel, then have some extra time at the world's largest field of gypsum sand dunes!"

In the backseat of the van, Benjamin buckled his seat belt and huddled into his damp sleeping bag. He didn't want to leave, but he couldn't help being excited about where they were going next. He'd read his guidebook carefully, so he knew a little bit about what to expect. New Mexico was one state with many different kinds of environments within it, and he couldn't wait to see the next one. By this time tomorrow, they'd be on the edge of the Chihuahuan Desert!

The next morning, Benjamin woke up in a dry motel, hardly remembering the drive from the Gila National Forest. He looked through the sliding-glass door of his family's motel room and wished everyone would wake up so they could go outside and look around!

His mom was the first adult up, and

he could swear she read his mind. Mrs. Baxter looked at the beds where Lucy and his dad were still conked out, and whispered, "Want to take a walk?" That's what they did back home in Florida when they got up early. It was a good way to look for local wildlife.

"I know we're near the Chihuahuan Desert, but where exactly are we?" Benjamin asked after they'd gotten dressed and left the motel.

"We're in the south-central part of the state, between White Sands and a town called Alamogordo," his mom replied. "If you look carefully, you can see the dunes that White Sands is named for out there." Sure enough, between the flat area of the town and the mountains in the distance was a strip of shimmering white that looked almost like snow. "I can't wait to see them in person!"

They continued walking, and before long, they were in a wide-open space. The ground was dry and brown, and where the Gila had been forested, there were now just small shrubs scattered all over the place. It was so different from the Gila National Forest that it was hard to believe they were in the same state.

"Is this the desert?" Benjamin asked as they walked into it. "Where's the tan, grainy sand? How about the giant cactuses?"

His mom smiled. "Not all deserts have sand and cactuses. Deserts come in many shapes and sizes, and this is one of them. It actually gets quite cold here in the winter—it's not as hot as deserts in other parts of the world. But, like all deserts, it receives hardly any rainfall. Any plant or animal that lives here must be able to withstand the very dry conditions."

Benjamin was still thinking about what wasn't there. "Like cactuses, right? They're perfect for the desert because they can hold water in their stems?"

"That's right," said his mom. "But they're not the only kind of plant that can do that. There are others, like the agave plant and the yucca. And animals have adaptations that allow them to live in the desert, too. Think of..."

His mom looked up and gasped. It was as if she had ordered a herd of animals to come running across the desert at just that moment. There, in front of the mountains, was what looked like a group of deer! ". . . pronghorn antelope!" she said.

"Antelope?" asked Benjamin, surprised. "I thought those were deer. Or goats, maybe." They were brown with white bellies, large eyes, and what appeared to be long horns curving forward over their heads.

"It's confusing," Beth Baxter said. "They're not really antelope, since antelope keep their horns forever, and pronghorns shed theirs. But what's really unusual about them is the way they're suited to this environment."

The pronghorns had stopped running. Now they were milling around, nibbling on the desert plants. They didn't look that dramatic to Benjamin.

"Next to cheetahs, they're the fastest animals on earth!" his mom said. "They can run up to sixty miles an hour—as fast as a car on a highway. And their vision is so good that it's often compared to how you'd see through a pair of high-power binoculars."

"That is so cool!" Benjamin said. "Still . . . what does that have to do with living in the desert?"

"With their speed, they can easily cover the vast amounts of territory in the desert," his mom explained. "They can go a long way for a meal. And with their vision, they can see predators coming a mile away. Speed and sight would come in handy anywhere, but especially here where the conditions are harsh."

Benjamin was still taking that in when his mom changed the subject. "You'll see many more desert animals this afternoon," she said. "I think that's enough science before breakfast, though. Let's get back and see if everyone else is awake."

Benjamin couldn't wait to tell Gabe and Lucy about the pronghorns, but they were talking so fast he couldn't get a word in edgewise. "We saw a roadrunner!" Gabe said. "Just a few minutes ago!"

For a moment, Benjamin thought they were talking about cartoons on TV. "Really?" Benjamin looked around the motel room. "Where?"

"Right here!" Lucy added. She was standing at the sliding door in Gabe's room, scanning the motel parking lot.

"Come with us to find it!" Gabe cried, practically pushing Benjamin out the door.

Their parents agreed they could go into the parking lot alone—since their rooms looked out onto it, they could keep an eye on the kids. Gabe led the way between some parked cars and onto a grassy median in front of the motel. From there, the three cousins could safely look across the rest of the lot and into the street that passed in front of it.

"There he is!" Gabe said, pointing enthusiastically.

The roadrunner was actually running in the road, chasing down something

they couldn't see. It had a black-and-white body and a crest of feathers on top of its head, bobbing as it ran. Its bill was large, its legs were long, and its tail was parallel to the ground as it dashed away. It reminded Benjamin of a very fast, very focused rooster!

"It's the state bird of New Mexico," he told Gabe and Lucy.

Lucy rolled her eyes. "You've been reading the guidebook again."

"They can fly, too," Gabe said, surprising Benjamin by knowing even more. "But they prefer to run or walk. They get around much faster on their feet. So fast, actually, that they can snatch certain prey out of the air."

Lucy looked at him curiously. "Have you been reading the book, too?" This was the first time their cousin had been able to inform them about an animal. "What do they eat?" she asked.

Gabe smiled. "Insects. Mice. And my favorite animals: scorpions and rattle-snakes."

"You keep finding animals on this trip. You'll be an expert before you know it," Lucy told him.

Gabe nodded, a big grin on his face. "I hope so!"

Chapter Five

At the White Sands Visitor Center, they picked up a new junior ranger booklet. Benjamin worked his way through a couple of puzzles right away, and he couldn't wait to start on the page called Animal Scavenger Hunt. What he was most excited about, though, was the last activity on the list: taking a sled ride down the dunes! The kids had picked up saucer sleds at the visitor center, too, and Benjamin couldn't wait to hit the slopes.

Right now, though, the sleds were piled under his feet in the van's backseat, and Benjamin couldn't keep his eyes off the scenery as Aunt Lily drove from the visitor center down a road that took them straight through a field of dunes as white as snow! The bright whiteness stretched for miles, ending only at the base of some faraway mountains. The only familiar thing in front of him was the road, and it was so hot that he felt like he was sitting in an oven. He'd never been anywhere quite like this, so open or so empty.

"What's the story?" Gabe asked. "Why does it look like this? It's like being on another planet or something."

Mr. Baxter tried to make it simple. "Those mountains in the distance contain an unusual mineral called gypsum. It dissolves in water, like sugar or salt, so rain washes it right off the rock and into this valley."

"There are no rivers here to take the rainwater—and gypsum—away," Benjamin's mom chimed in. "Instead, the water collects at the valley's lowest point. When it evaporates, all that's left are gypsum crystals. And the wind does a number on those, breaking them down into smaller and smaller pieces until they become the gypsum sand that you see."

"So this sand isn't like what you'd find at the beach?" asked Lucy.

"Well, it's kind of like regular sand," said Mr. Baxter. "All sand is made up of tiny pieces of different rocks and minerals. But here it's made only of pure gypsum, which is white."

"But we're still in the desert?" Gabe asked.

"Absolutely!" said Mrs. Baxter. "These dunes wouldn't exist without the dry climate of the desert. But the dunes present extra challenges to the plants and animals that live here. They need to cope with the desert climate as well as these huge stretches of white sand."

It was hard to imagine that anything lived here at all, Benjamin thought.

Benjamin, Lucy, and Gabe walked on a trail through the dunes, several yards ahead of their parents. In the dazzling sun, Lucy was squinting at the directions for the Animal Scavenger Hunt in their junior ranger booklet. "There are ten animals listed here, and we need to find at least three. If we do, we can get our junior ranger badges. But I don't know how we are going to find any of them," she said, looking around. "A lot of desert animals are nocturnal and try to avoid the heat of the day."

"We can still check them off the list if we see them sleeping," Benjamin said.

Then Gabe had a good idea. "There's some information about the animals in the booklet," he said. "Maybe if we use these facts like clues, we can find the animals. Like"—he leafed through the book—"the kangaroo rat . . . "

Benjamin looked at his booklet

and followed what Gabe was saying. "They burrow at the base of shrubs or bushes," he said. "Maybe if we find a burrow, we can find a rat?"

Lucy crouched down beside one of the few shrubs near the trail. Benjamin thought it might be another yucca. "Oh—there really is something here!" she cried.

Benjamin knelt down to take a look. He could see a small hole in the ground. "Do you think that's a burrow?"

"Well," Gabe said, "the kangaroo rat seals moisture into its burrow by plugging its entrance with soil." He was still reading from the booklet.

"So we can't see it unless we dig through the entrance?" Lucy asked, disappointed.

"I don't think we should do that,"

Benjamin said quickly. He hoped Gabe wouldn't mind, but there was no way they could destroy the animal's habitat.

"No problem," said Gabe. "But listen to this: Kangaroo rats can actually live without water! They save what they have; they seal themselves into the burrow, and they don't sweat or pant like other animals do to stay cool. But they also make water when they digest their food, which is mostly seeds! How cool is that?"

"That's some serious adaptation," Benjamin agreed.

"I wish it'd come out," Lucy said.

"Well, maybe we'll find another animal," Gabe said

Walking across the dunes was a strange sensation, Benjamin decided as they moved down the trail, the grown-ups still behind. Beneath the surface, the gypsum was almost solid. The top layer of the sand, though, was loose and grainy. After a while Benjamin also noticed that it was full of footprints! "Hey, you guys! Maybe we can track another animal this way," he said, pointing to the footprints.

"The only problem is that we don't know which animal made which tracks," Gabe said.

"I don't think it matters," Lucy said. "We can just follow one and see what we find!"

"Okay, but let's be careful," Gabe said.

Benjamin glanced back to make sure

the grown-ups were still in sight. The park's rules allowed people to venture off the trail, but cautioned that it was easy to get lost in the dunes. Benjamin figured they'd be fine if they didn't stray too far from their parents.

Crouching down, Gabe and Lucy followed a faint set of footprints, winding around clumps of wiry grass near the trail. The shape of the prints had been blurred by the wind shifting the sand, but it was clear that they belonged to some small animal, maybe a bird. Benjamin thought that they'd lead up to another burrow. He never expected they'd stumble across the animal itself!

But there it was, right out in the open. A totally ordinary lizard with one strange twist: It was white!

He waited for the grown-ups to catch up, then motioned them over. "What's this?" he asked. "An albino lizard?" Some people and animals were born without pigment in their skin, he knew. He'd never heard of that in a reptile, though.

"Or a ghost?" Gabe joked.

"A bleached earless lizard!" his dad said. "Amazing!"

"Another one from our list!" exclaimed Lucy, checking it off in her booklet. Then she grabbed her camera and began taking pictures of the unusual creature.

"This is the only place in the world that they live," his mom added. "There are other kinds of earless lizards—scientists think they evolved that way because of their habit of going headfirst into the ground—but only the white ones live in White Sands. Can anyone guess why?" she asked.

Gabe's hand shot into the air. "It has to be another adaptation! If they are white, they blend in with the sand and predators can't find them!"

"Their camouflage is so good that they can go out in the open like this, even in the middle of the day," Lucy added.

"Their color may even help them stay cooler, since white reflects the sun's light," said Mrs. Baxter. "Many other animals in White Sands have also developed lighter coloring, everything from mice to spiders."

At that moment, Benjamin happened to look down at his legs, which were turning pink in splotches. "It would be nice if we could evolve to survive here, too," he said. "Without worrying about sunscreen!"

After Benjamin's dad helped him reapply sun block, he said, "You kids ready to bring out the sleds?" They could return to the scavenger hunt later.

As they walked back to the car to get their rented sleds, Lucy did a happy dance, but Benjamin admitted something to Gabe as they were climbing to the top of a dune. "You know, I've never been sledding before! Unless you count being on a dogsled in Alaska. Do you know what to do?"

"Don't worry—just follow me," Gabe said, smiling. "I've been sledding tons of times in Central Park.

The only trick is not to go headfirst."

At the top of a tall dune, the kids got a panoramic view of the park. The sand was so white and he could see so

far that Benjamin could almost imagine he was standing at the North Pole (if he ignored the heat). He put his saucer sled near the edge of the dune, settled down, and pushed off with his hands. *Whoosh!*

On his next trip down, though, Benjamin's sled turned over near the bottom. He wasn't hurt, just startled. He sat on the harder sand at the base of the dune, watching Gabe and Lucy walk back up. Then something caught his eye.

He watched it until the other kids came back down. "Look! Over here!" he called to them. "I think I found a stinkbug!" He'd left his booklet in the car, but he remembered they were large and known for roaming randomly around their habitat. This one seemed to be walking around in circles!

Gabe pulled his junior ranger booklet out of his back pocket. "The darkling beetle," he read, "is about an inch long, smooth and black, with segmented antennae."

"Yep," said Benjamin. "That sounds right."

"No ability to fly," Gabe added.

"Looks like its wings are stuck together," Lucy reported.

"Also known as a stinkbug for its unusual way of defending itself. It raises its rear end and sprays a bad-smelling chemical!" Gabe finished up.

"The skunk of the desert," Benjamin said, laughing. "Better keep our distance!"

"Oh, definitely," Lucy said. "Because

now we've found three animals. And you know what that means, right? We missed our chance when we were at the Gila National Forest. But we can become junior rangers here, instead. We can finally get our badges!"

Chapter Six

The next morning, inside the visitor center, a ranger handed each of the cousins an embroidered badge. It showed an image of the dunes, with a yucca tree sticking out of the sand. Benjamin was already thinking about where he'd ask his mom to sew it for him. On his backpack, maybe? On the sleeve of his favorite jacket? He was so absorbed in the possibilities that he almost missed it when the ranger said, "Right this way, please."

Benjamin followed Gabe and Lucy into a large room with rows of seats and a big flag. "This is where we bring our tour groups for orientation," the ranger explained. "And also where we swear in our junior rangers. I'll recite the pledge line by line, and you can repeat after me."

Feeling like he was being sworn in for an important job, Benjamin repeated, "I promise to appreciate, respect, and protect all national parks. I also promise to continue learning about the landscape, plants, animals, and history of these special places. I will share what I learn with my friends and family."

The pledge reminded him of the

rules his family always tried to follow
when they were camping or exploring
nature: Be respectful. Leave nothing
behind. These were like second nature
to him. They were still new to Gabe,
though, and after the ranger handed

him his certificate, Gabe kept saying, "Wait till my friends back home hear about this!"

The families spent the evening back at the motel, swimming in the pool, and the next day they explored the area around White Sands. The following morning, Uncle Peter drove the van to their next stop, Carlsbad Caverns National Park, according to their original plan. They'd camp near the park for two days, and then it would be time for the cousins to fly home and get ready to go back to school. "I can't believe the trip is almost over," Lucy said sadly. "It feels like we just got started!"

They arrived at the campsite in the late afternoon, and this time the kids got to help pitch the tents. "Slide the poles in like this," Aunt Lily told Gabe. "Okay now . . . lift!" In a battered pot the Baxters had brought from home, they boiled water and cooked spaghetti over a blazing fire. It was camping just the way it was supposed to be, and Benjamin wished it would never end.

The next day, they set off to see Carlsbad Caverns. "There's a network of huge caves here, at least a hundred in the national park, plus hundreds more nearby," Benjamin said, reading from his guidebook on the ride to the caverns. "They were carved out of limestone by sulfuric acid millions of years ago. The limestone used to be part of a reef in an underground ocean! The caves are famous for their amazing rock formations and their colonies of Mexican free-tailed bats."

He couldn't wait to see the bats, although they wouldn't come out until sunset. But exploring the caves would be pretty cool, too. These weren't caves like they'd seen in the Gila, with large openings in the front. They were so deep underground that people had never lived in them. This part of New Mexico was also desert, like the part around White Sands, but the many caves set it apart and drew more tourists.

When they approached the main entrance to the caves, Mr. Baxter gathered everyone around. "We have two choices here," he said. "We can take an elevator to the visitor center at the bottom, or we can walk down on our own. It's about seventy-nine stories."

"Hey, that's more than half as tall as the Empire State Building," Gabe chimed in.

"And it's a steep climb, but that way we can see the passages and formations along the way."

"Walk!" the kids said together.

"We can always take the elevator back," Mrs. Baxter said.

It was dark and cool inside the caves, and the air felt damp. The trail descended at a steep angle, and Benjamin couldn't see what lay ahead, since it took so many turns. "Are we almost at the bottom? he asked as they walked. "How long does it take to climb down seventy-nine stories?"

After climbing for what seemed like

hours, Aunt Lily finally called out, "We're almost there!"

As they walked, Benjamin noticed the rock formations called stalactites reaching down from the ceiling, plus stalagmites reaching up from the floor, all in weird shapes, all glowing

in the eerie light inside the cave. "There's the Witch's Finger!" Gabe's dad said, reading a tourist brochure he had picked up and pointing at a thin pillar of stone, standing alone along the path. They also passed through the Devil's Den, where the path seemed to go straight down to the center of the earth, and the Devil's Spring, where a fringe of thin rock strands stretched out over an underground pond.

"I wonder where the bats are," Benjamin mumbled to Gabe. He was trying to focus on the animals they'd see, not the rock formations.

"Hey—are you okay?" said his cousin. "You've been a little quieter than usual."

"It feels strange to be so far underground," Benjamin admitted. He didn't like being inside quite as much as he had expected to.

"Stick with me," Gabe said. "This is one thing I'm really used to. I mean . . . think of the New York subway system! If that's not underground, I don't know what is."

Benjamin smiled as he followed his cousin all the way down to the Big Room, the largest underground chamber. It was as big as six football fields, filled with intricate patterns of rock and giant, stony domes. Even Benjamin had to admit it was magnificent. He wondered what it must have felt like to be the first human being to discover it. Now that would be some cool exploring, he thought. Well worth the long trip into the ground.

* * *

By the time they came out of the cave, blinking in the light, it was getting close to sunset. The two families left the park for dinner, then came back for the evening bat flight program given by a park ranger. Benjamin could hardly sit still outside the cave entrance, where about a hundred folding chairs had been set up. Finally, the park ranger came to tell them a little bit about what they were going to see.

"The Carlsbad Caverns are home to about half a million bats," she said. "And every evening they exit through a narrow passageway to look for food. Does anybody know what they eat?" she asked the audience.

"Blood!" yelled a boy sitting in front of Benjamin.

The ranger laughed. "It's a common

misconception that bats are danger-ous," she said. "But, in fact, only one kind of bat, the vampire bat, sucks blood from other animals. Bats are the only mammal that can fly, and this allows them to eat something else, a kind of food that other mammals can't reach."

Lucy raised her hand, and the ranger called on her next. "Most bats eat insects," she said. "Since they can fly, they can catch them in midair. But insects don't live in caves. That's why the bats have to leave."

"That's right," the ranger said. "Bats are important because they help keep insect populations under control, especially out in the desert. Here's another interesting thing about them: Like other animals in this climate, bats are nocturnal. They have an unusual ability that allows them to see well in the dark. Does anybody know what it is?"

This time she called on Uncle Peter. "Would that be echolocation?" he said.

"Absolutely," the ranger said. "When they are hunting for food—or just trying to find their way at night—bats send sounds out into the air around them. When the sounds bounce back, they can judge where an object—or prey—is as well as how fast it is moving. They 'see' the object without using their eyes."

A murmur spread through the audience. While the ranger was talking, a dark cloud began to form above the caves. "The bats are starting to come out!" Lucy exclaimed.

Benjamin watched, astonished, as the cloud of bats grew bigger and darker. "They fly in a spiral," the ranger explained. "And then they break off from the group to find their dinner.

Sometimes this flight takes twenty minutes—sometimes it takes two hours!"

"How do they know when it's time to go?" Benjamin asked. "I mean, it's dark in the cave—they can't tell when the sun is starting to set, can they?

Mrs. Baxter shook her head. "Scientists have asked that same question," she replied. "But nobody knows for sure yet."

The bats were so small, and there were so many of them, that Benjamin couldn't get a good sense of what an individual bat looked like. He would have to search for more information in his guidebook, or maybe at home. He had a great sense, though, of what amazing creatures they were, and how glad he was to be able to see them leave the cave like this. In his dad's brochure, he'd noticed that some mornings there was also an early-morning program where people could see the bats return to the cave for the day. He wished they could do that, too, but he had a feeling that nobody else would want to be awake before sunrise!

That night, he lay awake in the tent long after Gabe and Lucy had gone to sleep. He always hated the end of a trip, even though he knew he'd be happy at home with his friends and his dog. No trip ever seemed long enough, and even though he'd seen lots of animals over the last few days, he always wished he could see more.

There are animals at home, too, he reminded himself. People traveled from all over to visit the Everglades, and that's where he lived all the time! School would be starting soon, with homework and soccer practice and birthday parties. Benjamin liked all that stuff, but he didn't like that it could get in the way of exploring nature. He promised himself that he'd make more time for observing the world around him.

The words of the junior ranger pledge rang in his ears as he finally drifted off to sleep. "I promise to continue learning . . . I promise to share what I learn with my friends and family."

The trip had been the perfect combination of family fun and learning. On the tiny glimpse of the full moon he could see through the window in his tent, he wished that the Baxters and the Sullivans would take another trip like this again soon!

Meet the Baxters as they explore
Brooklyn in Book 1 of the
JUNIOR EXPLORER SERIES.

And read more of the Baxter kids'
adventures in the second book of the series!